SEXUAL INTEGRITY
Balancing Your Passion
with Purity

JUNE HUNT

ROSE PUBLISHING/ASPIRE PRESS

Torrance, California

ROSE PUBLISHING/ASPIRE PRESS

CONTENTS

ear friend,

Never will I forget being stunned by these words—profound words that to this day are seared in my memory:

"Sin will make you stray further than you thought you'd stray.

Sin will make you stay longer than you thought you'd stay.

Sin will make you pay more than you thought you'd pay."

Oh, how true! Over the years, these words have continued to ring in my ears—especially as I've thought about my own life. I remember making choices in my early life that I wish I could remake. And those wrong choices only reinforce the fact of that first refrain, *"Sin will make you stray further than you thought you'd stray."*

For that matter, every person alive can attest to the truth of these words when they examine their own lives. (And I'm confident that if it were possible to poll the dead, a unanimous "Amen" would ring out from the grave!) Certain great leaders, even spiritual leaders, know the reality of letting down their guard.

When we think of David in the Bible, we are drawn to him—we feel with him. Perhaps it's because in some ways, we are like him.

Remember the evening on the rooftop of the palace when King David saw a beautiful woman bathing? At that moment, he had the choice to look away and not give in to lust. Instead, even after discovering that she was married, David opened the door to sexual passion and strayed away from the truth he well knew. He called for her, slept with her, and she conceived.

Undoubtedly, David stayed longer than he thought he'd stay. In order to hide his sexual tryst, David, in essence, had her husband killed on the battlefield. Although David did marry Bathsheba, he certainly learned that sin made him pay more than he thought he'd pay. Six days after the birth of their baby, their little son died. God's hand of blessing was not on David at that point in his life because he failed to be a man of sexual integrity. (See 2 Samuel 11–12:23.)

You have a major decision to make, and no one can make it for you. The question to ask yourself is this: *Am I willing to be a person of sexual integrity?* I beg you to answer yes—for your sake—and then put action steps in place to secure your decision. Repeatedly, throughout your lifetime, you will be faced with this same question, *Am I willing to be a person of sexual integrity?* The steps contained within this book will be of immense help to keep you on track—to keep you from straying.

And if, based on your past, you may have any doubt about being successful, I give you this assurance: *You can be a person of sexual integrity.* When you allow Christ to take control of your life, the Bible says, *"The one who calls you is faithful and he will do it"* (1 Thessalonians 5:24).

Yours in the Lord's hope,

June Hunt

P.S. Let this be your daily prayer: *"I seek you with all my heart; do not let me stray from your commands."* (Psalm 119:10)

SEXUAL INTEGRITY
Balancing Your Passion with Purity

He had it all! He had the call of God, the anointing of God, the blessing of God, and the power of God—all at his fingertips. He had every opportunity to live an exemplary life—to be a hero throughout the annals of history.

His parents established a positive home environment. They were sure he would be a strong leader—indeed, his extraordinary feats made him famous. But in spite of great ability and great advantage, his moral failure led to his downfall.

Throughout history, this infamous man will be remembered for both his immense strength and his immense weakness.

How different the life of Samson could have been! If only he had withstood the test of sexual integrity—if only he had not succumbed to the lure of sexual seduction—a lure that led to his ultimate destruction. Yet, instead of obedience, he chose disobedience; instead of self-denial, he chose self-indulgence.

"He [Samson] fell in love with a woman ... whose name was Delilah. The rulers of the Philistines went to her and said, 'See if you can lure him into showing you the secret of his great strength and how we can overpower him so we may tie him up and subdue him.'"
(Judges 16:4–5)

DEFINITIONS

Samson was God's chosen leader to deliver God's chosen people from the oppression of the Philistines. Before his birth, the angel of the Lord had announced to his parents that their son would be a judge over the Israelites, but warned that he should not cut his hair, for if he did, he would lose his strength.

However, instead of living to please his God, Samson lived to please himself. Rather than learning to exercise the discipline of *delayed gratification* (waiting until the right time and the right circumstance to do what is pleasurable), Samson insisted on *instant gratification*. Even in his early manhood, his mother and father appealed to their son.

"His father and mother replied,
'Isn't there an acceptable woman ...
among all our people?
Must you go to the uncircumcised
Philistines to get a wife?'
But Samson said to his father,
'Get her for me.
She's the right one for me.'"
(Judges 14:3)

WHAT IS Sexual Integrity?

We love our heroes. We need heroes in every generation and in every culture: heroes who possess what they profess, who reflect what they represent, who walk their talk, and who survive close scrutiny. True heroes have integrity and are worthy of imitation. We find hope in heroes who are willing to stand alone regardless of stress, who hold to principle no matter the pressure, and who will not compromise their convictions. One aspect of the overall integrity of true heroes is their sexual integrity.

▶ **Sexual integrity** is consistently living your life according to the highest moral sexual standards—consistently guarding your mind, will, and emotions from sexual impurity.

"The man of integrity walks securely, but he who takes crooked paths will be found out." (Proverbs 10:9)

▶ The word *integrity* means whole, undivided, and void of hypocrisy. Those who have integrity complete their commitments. The Old Testament Hebrew word translated "integrity" is *tom*, which means "to be complete, to finish."[1]

11

"Righteousness guards the man of integrity, but wickedness overthrows the sinner." (Proverbs 13:6)

▶ **Sexual integrity** is to be the same in the dark as you are in the light—not double-minded with contradictory thoughts, words, and deeds. The person without integrity ...

"... is a double-minded man, unstable in all he does." (James 1:8)

WHAT IS Sexual Enticement?

A true hunter thinks nothing of sitting camouflaged in the bare branches of a tree battling freezing weather through a wintry night, sometimes enticing his prized game with bait or a "call." He hunts for the love of the sport and sometimes for the trophy on the wall.

Whether the sexual hunt is for sport or for seduction, this hunter gives great thought to just the right location and the most effective approach. Just as Samson was Delilah's trophy, you may have been the victim of a sexual hunt—the trophy of someone's sexual conquest. If so, you know the power and pull of sexual enticement.

▶**Sexual enticement** is an *erotic temptation*, a passionate attraction. By God's design, sexual desire is normal, natural, and good. Although God designed sex, He does not tempt you with sex. The Bible says ...

"When tempted, no one should say, 'God is tempting me.' For God cannot be tempted by evil, nor does he tempt anyone." (James 1:13)

▶**Sexual enticement** is an *internal temptation* that occurs when something or someone is alluring to you. In the New Testament the Greek word *deleazo* comes from an old hunting and fishing term that means "to lure by a bait" and is translated "to tempt or entice."[2]

"Each one is tempted when, by his own evil desire, he is dragged away and enticed." (James 1:14)

▶**Sexual enticement** is an *external temptation* that occurs when someone attempts to lure you. In the Old Testament the Hebrew word *patah* means "to entice, deceive, or persuade."[3] Remember ...

"If sinners entice you, do not give in to them." (Proverbs 1:10)

QUESTION: "Is sexual temptation a sin?"

ANSWER: No. Temptation is not a sin, but to yield to temptation is a sin. We are all tempted in different areas. The issue is whether we give in to temptation or not. Only one person on earth experienced temptation in every area, yet was without sin—Jesus, our Savior.

> "We do not have a high priest who is unable to sympathize with our weaknesses, but we have one who has been tempted in every way, just as we are—yet was without sin."
> (Hebrews 4:15)

Biblical Examples of Sexual Enticement

▶ **Flirtation**

Salome danced enticingly for Herod.

Read Matthew chapter 14.

▶ **Seduction**

Potiphar's wife sought to seduce Joseph.

Read Genesis chapter 39.

▶ **Lust**

Samson lusted after Delilah.

Read Judges chapter 16.

▶ Adultery

David committed adultery with Bathsheba.

Read 2 Samuel chapter 11.

▶ Promiscuity

The woman at the well lived in sin with a man who was not her husband.

Read John chapter 4.

▶ Homosexuality

Homosexual men lusted after the visitors in Lot's home.

Read Genesis chapter 19.

▶ Incest

Lot's two daughters tricked him into getting drunk and had sexual relations with him.

Read Genesis chapter 19.

▶ Rape

Amnon raped his half sister Tamar.

Read 2 Samuel chapter 13.

QUESTION: "Am I obligated to give sexual favors to someone who has spent money on me by buying me jewelry, taking me to dinner, going to the theater, or paying my rent?"

ANSWER: No. You are worth far more than any gift, favor, or dollar amount. You are made in the image of God, and it is far beneath your dignity to perform any type of sexual favor in return for any type of gift or "investment." Stop and realize how valuable you are before bartering yourself for anyone or anything. The Bible says ...

> "The body is not meant for sexual immorality, but for the Lord, and the Lord for the body."
> (1 Corinthians 6:13)

Remember your first real crush? The flush of your face, the pounding of your heart, the shortness of breath at your first touch? You were "in love" or perhaps, more realistically, in love with love. Your heart was filled with excitement at the anticipation of holding hands and receiving a sweet goodnight kiss.

Such were the days of innocence—the ways of "puppy love." But when infatuation turns to feverish passion, innocence can be lost. What you think is love turns out to be lust, an *illusion* of true intimacy, a *counterfeit* of the lasting love that sustains a relationship. Too late, you may learn there are great differences between lust and love.

The Bible tells us ...

> **"Put to death, therefore, whatever belongs to your earthly nature: sexual immorality, impurity, lust, evil desires and greed, which is idolatry."**
> **(Colossians 3:5)**

> **"I tell you that anyone who looks at a woman lustfully has already committed adultery with her in his heart."**
> **(Matthew 5:28)**

Lust Is:	Love Is:
Temporary	Enduring
Sudden	Gradual
Selfish	Unselfish
Untrustworthy	Trustworthy
Impatient	Patient
Faithless	Faithful
Uncontrolled desire	Controlled desire
Emotionally shallow	Emotionally deep
Based on fantasy	Based on reality
Full of emotion	Full of devotion
Driven by one's passion	Chosen by one's will
Focused on external looks	Focused on internal character
Established on faulty reasoning	Established on solid reasoning
Set on getting happiness	Set on giving happiness
Eager to get	Eager to give

"Love is patient, love is kind.
It does not envy, it does not boast,
it is not proud. It is not rude, it is not
self-seeking, it is not easily angered, it
keeps no record of wrongs.
Love does not delight in evil but rejoices
with the truth. It always protects,
always trusts, always hopes, always
perseveres. Love never fails."
(1 Corinthians 13:4–8)

Have you ever gazed into the clean, clear water of a still, pristine lake? Its unsoiled beauty encourages us to appreciate the purity of God's initial design. And just as beautiful are two sexually pure lives that come together for physical fulfillment within the marriage relationship. Such purity is attainable, even if, at one time, it had been lost. Yes, even if you have suffered from a past of sexual impurity, through the power of God that which is impure can once again become spiritually clean.

The Bible says ...

**"Let us draw near to God with a sincere heart in full assurance of faith, having our hearts sprinkled to cleanse us from a guilty conscience and having our bodies washed with pure water."
(Hebrews 10:22)**

▶ **Sexual purity** is chastity or freedom from sexually immoral attitudes and actions. We are told ...

"Set an example for the believers in speech, in life, in love, in faith and in purity."
(1 Timothy 4:12)

▶ **Sexual purity** doesn't "just happen." Because of our bent to sin, we need to take an active role in purifying our hearts, which will in turn purify our attitudes and actions.

The Bible says ...

"Come near to God and he will come near to you. Wash your hands, you sinners, and purify your hearts, you double-minded." (James 4:8)

▶ The Greek word *hagnos* means "pure from defilement." This word is derived from *hagios*, signifying "holy," "pure," and "being set apart."[4] This is why the Bible says ...

"Among you there must not be even a hint of sexual immorality, or of any kind of impurity, or of greed, because these are improper for God's holy people." (Ephesians 5:3)

Joseph: A Biblical Example of Sexual Purity

"He [Potiphar] left in Joseph's care everything he had; with Joseph in charge, he did not concern himself with anything except the food he ate. Now Joseph was well-built and handsome, and after a while his master's wife took notice of Joseph and said, 'Come to bed with me!' But he refused. 'With me in charge,' he told her, 'my master does not concern himself with anything in the house; everything he owns he has entrusted to my care. No one is greater in this house than I am. My master has withheld nothing from me except you, because you are his wife. How then could I do such a wicked thing and sin against God?' And though she spoke to Joseph day after day, he refused to go to bed with her or even be with her. One day he went into the house to attend to his duties, and none of the household servants was inside. She caught him by his cloak and said, 'Come to bed with me!' But he left his cloak in her hand and ran out of the house." (Genesis 39:6–12)

You don't have to go far in the Bible to learn God's heart on healthy sexual relationships. The first four points of His plan are mentioned in the second chapter of Genesis, and this blueprint, repeated in the New Testament, demonstrates God's desire for us to get it right!

> **""Haven't you read," he [Jesus] replied, "that at the beginning the Creator 'made them male and female,' and said, 'For this reason a man will leave his father and mother and be united to his wife, and the two will become one flesh'"?"**
> **(Matthew 19:4–5)**

1. **The man and the woman will establish a separate family unit from their parents.**

   "For this reason a man will leave his father and mother ..." (Genesis 2:24)

2. **The married couple will cleave, unite, bond to each other as the priority relationship.**

   "... and be united to his wife ..." (Genesis 2:24)

3. **The "one flesh" sexual relationship will begin *after* the God-ordained marriage between husband and wife.**

   " ... and they will become one flesh" (Genesis 2:24)

4. The sexual and emotional intimacy in marriage will be open and vulnerable with moral purity between husband and wife.

"The man and his wife were both naked, and they felt no shame." (Genesis 2:25)

5. Marriage partners will not be burdened by the fear or shame of pregnancy out of wedlock.

"God blessed them and said to them, 'Be fruitful and increase in number.'" (Genesis 1:28)

6. The intimate relationship will represent the intimate oneness that true believers have with the Lord.

"As a bridegroom rejoices over his bride, so will your God rejoice over you." (Isaiah 62:5)

CHARACTERISTICS OF SEXUAL INTEGRITY VS. SEXUAL IMMORALITY

Samson—what a tower of strength—a tower reduced to rubble! Rather than living a life of self-sacrifice, he is consumed with self-centeredness. Rather than following God's instruction about "unclean" food, he consumes the forbidden food (eating honey from the carcass of a lion). Rather than seeking justice for the Lord's sake, he seeks revenge for his own sake. Rather than finding a godly wife, he focuses on ungodly women. His frequent lust for sexually "forbidden fruit" is not just a simple character flaw in one area of his life, but rather a symptom of a corrupt character affecting all areas of his life. (See Judges 14:8–9; 15:3; 16:1.)

The Bible says ...

> "To those who are corrupted and do not believe, nothing is pure. In fact, both their minds and consciences are corrupted."
> (Titus 1:15)

No comparison has more contrast than that of the exemplary life of Joseph and the carnal life of Samson. Both are divinely chosen deliverers of Israel, but at the same time, moral opposites. Joseph is faithful in his service and practices self-control. Samson merely follows his passions with no self-control. Joseph is remembered for "forgiving his enemy," whereas Samson is known for "sleeping with the enemy." Joseph begins his adulthood as a slave and rises to the top, whereas Samson begins at the top and spirals down into slavery—a slave to immorality and a slave to the Philistines. What a stark contrast!

Their lives poignantly represent the contrast in this proverb:

> **"The righteousness of the upright delivers them, but the unfaithful are trapped by evil desires."**
> **(Proverbs 11:6)**

A Contrast in Character

▶ **Joseph:** Sexual Integrity

Genesis chapters 37–50

▶ **Samson:** Sexual Immorality

Judges chapters 13–16

▶ **Joseph will not violate God's commands**, though his decision costs him his freedom.

"No one is greater in this house than I am. My master has withheld nothing from me except you, because you are his wife. How then could I do such a wicked thing and sin against God?" (Genesis 39:9)

▶ **Samson violates God's commands** and satisfies his sexual lust.

"Samson went down to Timnah and saw there a young Philistine woman." (Judges 14:1)

▶ **Joseph purposely avoids sexually tempting situations.**

"Though she spoke to Joseph day after day, he refused to go to bed with her or even be with her." (Genesis 39:10)

▶ **Samson purposely avails himself of sexually tempting situations.**

"One day Samson went to Gaza, where he saw a prostitute. He went in to spend the night with her." (Judges 16:1)

▶ **Joseph flees illicit sex** from a conniving woman.

"She caught him by his cloak and said, 'Come to bed with me!' But he left his cloak in her hand and ran out of the house." (Genesis 39:12)

▶ **Samson seeks illicit sex** from seductive women.

"One day Samson went to Gaza, where he saw a prostitute. He went in to spend the night with her." (Judges 16:1)

▶ **Joseph focuses on the needs of others.**

"I will provide for you there, because five years of famine are still to come. Otherwise you and your household and all who belong to you will become destitute." (Genesis 45:11)

▶ **Samson focuses on his own desires.**

"Some time later, he fell in love with a woman in the Valley of Sorek whose name was Delilah." (Judges 16:4)

▶ **Joseph's life is preserved** because he humbly pursues morality.

"God sent me ahead of you to preserve for you a remnant on earth and to save your lives by a great deliverance." (Genesis 45:7)

▶ **Samson's life is destroyed** because he arrogantly pursues immorality.

"Then she called, 'Samson, the Philistines are upon you!' He awoke from his sleep and thought, 'I'll go out as before and shake myself free.' But he did not know that the Lord had left him." (Judges 16:20)

▶ **Joseph refuses to seek personal revenge.**

"He kissed all his brothers and wept over them. Afterward his brothers talked with him." (Genesis 45:15)

▶ **Samson seeks personal revenge.**

"Samson said to them, 'This time I have a right to get even with the Philistines; I will really harm them.'" (Judges 15:3)

▶ **Joseph brings honor to his parents.**

"Joseph settled his father and his brothers in Egypt and gave them property in the best part of the land, the district of Rameses, as Pharaoh directed." (Genesis 47:11)

▶ **Samson brings dishonor to his parents.**

"His father and mother replied, 'Isn't there an acceptable woman among your relatives or among all our people? Must you go to the uncircumcised Philistines to get a wife?' But Samson said to his father, 'Get her for me. She's the right one for me.'" (Judges 14:3)

Both Joseph and Samson were indeed deliverers. Joseph delivered Israel as an extraordinary man of integrity during his life. Samson delivered Israel as an imprisoned blind man by his death. (See Judges 16:21–30.)

WHAT CHARACTERIZES Those Ensnared in Sexual Sin?

We all have heard people say, "I didn't realize I was getting into a bad relationship. I didn't see the trouble down the road."

Yet sometimes we choose to be blind to the obvious. We refuse to see the negative because we don't want to give up the relationship.

Samson was one man who chose his own blindness. On numerous occasions, Delilah had been deceitful, and Samson knew it. But he chose to ignore the obvious and to foolishly disclose to her the secret of his great strength. Ultimately, he chose to be ensnared. In truth, he could agree with the following words of warning because they tragically reflect his own downfall:

"I find more bitter than death the woman who is a snare, whose heart is a trap and whose hands are chains.
The man who pleases God will escape her, but the sinner she will ensnare."
(Ecclesiastes 7:26)

Characteristics of Those Ensnared in Sexual Sin (from Romans 1 and the book of Proverbs):

▶ **Foolish**

"Although they claimed to be wise, they became fools." (Romans 1:22)

"She gives no thought to the way of life." (Proverbs 5:6)

▶ **Undisciplined**

"God gave them over in the sinful desires of their hearts to sexual impurity for the degrading of their bodies with one another." (Romans 1:24)

"She is undisciplined and without knowledge." (Proverbs 9:13)

▶ **Lustful and Seductive**

"God gave them over to shameful lusts." (Romans 1:26)

"With persuasive words she led him astray; she seduced him with her smooth talk." (Proverbs 7:21)

▶ **Defiant**

"They have become filled with every kind of wickedness, evil, greed and depravity." (Romans 1:29)

"She is loud and defiant, her feet never stay at home." (Proverbs 7:11)

▶ Deceitful

"They are full of envy, murder, strife, deceit and malice." (Romans 1:29)

"Her paths are crooked, but she knows it not." (Proverbs 5:6)

▶ Conniving

"They invent ways of doing evil." (Romans 1:30)

"Then out came a woman to meet him, dressed like a prostitute and with crafty intent." (Proverbs 7:10)

▶ Bitter

"They are gossips, slanderers, God-haters, insolent, arrogant and boastful." (Romans 1:29–30)

"In the end she is bitter as gall, sharp as a double-edged sword." (Proverbs 5:4)

▶ Boastful

"They are ... boastful." (Romans 1:29–30)

"The woman Folly is loud; she is undisciplined and without knowledge." (Proverbs 9:13)

▶ Unfaithful

"They are senseless, faithless, heartless, ruthless." (Romans 1:31)

"[She] has left the partner of her youth and ignored the covenant she made before God." (Proverbs 2:17)

▶ Unashamed

"They are ... heartless, ruthless." (Romans 1:31)

"She eats and wipes her mouth and says, 'I've done nothing wrong.'" (Proverbs 30:20)

QUESTION: "My ex-wife was sexually involved with another man while we were married. I knew she was promiscuous before we got married, but why would she devalue our marriage?"

ANSWER: Marriage is not a cure for all problems. The problems that exist in a relationship prior to marriage will also present themselves in the marriage. You need to attain freedom from the emotional damage you experienced. Choose to forgive your ex-wife. Pray that you will grow in wisdom and that you will learn to discern the character of people before entering into a relationship with them. Unmarried men and women who value the sanctity of marriage keep themselves pure and avoid promiscuity. Marriage does not change a person's character.

"The wisdom of the prudent is to give thought to their ways, but the folly of fools is deception." (Proverbs 14:8)

CAUSES OF VULNERABILITY

What led Samson into a life of moral failure? While he relied on God for his physical strength, he failed to rely on God for his moral strength. Samson assumed that God would continue to give him extraordinary strength regardless of his disobedience. Clearly, God gave Samson the supernatural strength needed to defeat the Philistines. But Samson never saw his need for strength of character. Because of the womanly wiles of Delilah, he compromised his convictions by telling her the secret of his great strength. In time, Samson's lack of character cost him not only his liberty, but his life.

"Then she called, 'Samson, the Philistines are upon you!' He awoke from his sleep and thought, 'I'll go out as before and shake myself free.' But he did not know that the Lord had left him. Then the Philistines seized him, gouged out his eyes and took him down to Gaza. Binding him with bronze shackles, they set him to grinding in the prison. ... Samson said, 'Let me die with the Philistines!' Then he pushed with all his might, and down came the temple on the rulers and all the people in it. Thus he killed many more when he died than while he lived." (Judges 16:20–21, 30)

Many people offer many reasons for "giving in" to the pressure of sex outside of marriage. These reasons—called excuses—are as varied as the people themselves, and yet they are all too common because they have been used since the beginning of time.

Whatever "reason" is presented, the reality is that we—like Samson—want to live according to our own desires, not in obedience to God, who created us as sexual beings with His plan and purpose. He knows far better than we how to *satisfy* our God-designed, God-given sexual needs.

> "The LORD will guide you always;
> he will satisfy your needs in a
> sun-scorched land
> and will strengthen your frame.
> You will be like a well-watered garden,
> like a spring whose waters never fail."
> (Isaiah 58:11)

Twelve "Reasons"

▶ **"He says that if I don't have sex, he will find someone else who will."**

If he is willing to have sex with anyone available, then he has no commitment to you. This is not a person who cares about you.

▶ **"I don't like being teased because I won't do it."**

A person who teases you because you won't have sex doesn't respect your standards and is trying to manipulate you into lowering them.

▶ **"I can hold on to him if I have sex with him."**

Don't allow yourself to be that desperate. You are more valuable than that. If that's the only way to hold on to someone, then you really do not want that person.

▶ **"I'm just curious."**

You can be curious about many things, but the appropriate time for a sexual relationship is within a committed marriage relationship. If you put your trust in God's timing, your curiosity will give way to contentment.

▶ **"I'm lonely."**

A sexual experience is not the cure for loneliness. In fact, you may feel even more isolated after a casual sexual encounter—all alone with guilt and regret.

▶ **"It's not my fault if I'm drunk."**

Any drink or drug that impairs your judgment is not safe. Decide today not to drink anything that weakens your defenses.

▶ **"I'll use a condom. It's safe sex."**

No contraceptive is 100% effective, and no "protection" can guarantee safety from sexually transmitted diseases (STDs)— except abstinence. Condoms can slip, leak, and break—that's not safe sex. Even if you use a condom, you face the possibility of emotional and physical damage from the sexual encounter that can last a lifetime.

▶ **"I just want to feel loved."**

A sexual relationship without commitment is not based on love but on lust. Sex is not love, and love is not sex. Animals have sex with no commitment of love, whereas humans need a relationship based on love.

▶ **"I just want to get it over with."**

If you "just want to get it over with," you are being pressured into doing something that you don't want to do—so don't do it!

▶ "I don't want to be the last one to have sex."

Be concerned with your own choices, not with those of everyone else. Half the teens in America between the ages of 15 and 19 are virgins. Being the first or the last is not the issue—obeying God is what's important.

▶ "I don't want to look like a prude."

Submission to the standards of your Creator is more important than meeting the expectations of your culture. By being sexually pure, you will be a testimony to others facing the same choices you are facing.

▶ "I was sexually abused as a child, so it doesn't matter."

Your decision about whether or not to have sex outside of marriage matters to God. Although you were sexually violated, being victimized was not your choice, nor was it your fault! God sees you, if you are a believer, as unblemished and pure, and He will empower you to stay sexually pure. It matters from this day forward that you live a life of sexual purity.

As you nurture a "family of friends" and look for ways to regularly serve others, you will find yourself focused not on sex, but on loving others with a pure heart.

> **"You ... were called to be free.
> But do not use your freedom to indulge
> the sinful nature; rather, serve
> one another in love."**
> **(Galatians 5:13)**

QUESTION: "How should I respond when I know I'm attracted to someone who is wrong for me?"

ANSWER: Ranchers know that to keep horses in a corral, the gate must be kept shut. Once the gate is open, the horses run out. This same principle applies to your emotions. If you keep the door shut on your wrong desires and refuse to open the door to wrong relationships, then you have kept rein on your emotions and have "guarded your heart."

Pray, "Lord, I thank You for giving me wisdom to know that this attraction is wrong for me. With Your strength, I choose to guard my heart and to focus only on Your perfect will for my life."

The Bible says ...

> **"Above all else, guard your heart,
> for it is the wellspring of life."**
> **(Proverbs 4:23)**

Many people become vulnerable to sexual pressure because of never having moved through the developmental stages of childhood in a healthy way. Something or someone was missing. But all is not lost. God can use our past pain to open our hearts, teach us wisdom, and bring healing into our lives.

> "Surely you desire truth in the inner parts; you teach me wisdom in the inmost place."
> (Psalm 51:6)

1 Lack of **Self-worth**

Self-worth is an inner God-given trait that parents should cultivate in their children. If we have a lack of self-worth, instead of looking to God to confer His value on us, we often look to another person to give us a sense of worth.

▶ Those who want to bolster their self-worth may assume that engaging in sex is the solution to their problems. But to grasp our true meaning and purpose, we must realize that God has already established our worth.

▶ When sex outside of marriage causes self-worth to plummet further, the false assumption can be, *I'll feel better about myself if I have more sex.* However, instead of turning to sex to establish our value, we must remember we are so valuable that God has already planned a positive future for us. The Bible says ...

"'I know the plans I have for you,' declares the LORD, 'plans to prosper you and not to harm you, plans to give you hope and a future.'" (Jeremiah 29:11)

2 Lack of **Self-control**

Self-control is a personal trait that should be developed at an early age—a discipline necessary throughout your lifetime.

▶ The toddler who was never taught to stay out of the cookie jar before dinner will have difficulty moving into the teenage years because of a lack of self-control.

▶ When the flames of sexual desires begin to burn out of control, the undisciplined person does not possess the necessary control to put out the fire. If you struggle with lack of self-control, the Bible gives this warning:

"Like a city whose walls are broken down is a man who lacks self-control." (Proverbs 25:28)

3 Lack of **Self-respect**

Self-respect is a character trait that should be nurtured in childhood by your parents and all extended family members. Children learn to respect themselves and others from the way they are treated at home.

▶ If family members have not treated you with respect, you can still gain self-respect by believing and accepting the love God has for you and accepting the value He has placed on you. People are His most special creation, fashioned in His very image.

▶ Refraining from having sex outside of marriage shows true respect for yourself, respect for the one you date, and respect for your future mate.

"Show proper respect to everyone: Love the brotherhood of believers, fear God, honor the king." (1 Peter 2:17)

4 Lack of **Emotional Intimacy**

Emotional intimacy is a need that all children, teens, and adults have—a need for emotional closeness with others. When a parent is emotionally distant, children are unable to develop the healthy attachments necessary for secure, stable, adult relationships.

▶ Lack of emotional intimacy cultivates ground for unhealthy, codependent, needy relationships.

▶ To compensate for the emotional void, many people develop intense emotional attachments that become fertile soil for unhealthy sexual relationships, including even same-sex sexual attractions. Regardless of our background, we all need to experience the unchanging love of the Lord.

God assures us, "I have loved you with an everlasting love; I have drawn you with loving-kindness." (Jeremiah 31:3)

5 Lack of **Communication**

Communication is learned by children primarily at home. When communication exists on only superficial levels, children are unable to express their natural questions and feelings about sexuality. One of the major factors in determining our attitudes about sex and morals is whether our parents have openly communicated their attitudes and morals.

▶ Although many parents shy away from using the word "sex," hoping that their children will somehow learn about sex without home discussions, all children should be taught the truth about sexuality.

▶ All young people should be trained in how to make right decisions about sex. Otherwise, when they are faced with making choices in the heat of passion, their decisions will be based on *feelings* rather than on *fact*. They are not likely to have the reasons or the readiness to say *no* when needed.

"It [the grace of God] teaches us to say 'No' to ungodliness and worldly passions, and to live self-controlled, upright and godly lives in this present age." (Titus 2:12)

6 Lack of **Boundaries**

Boundaries are a child's first line of defense against outside danger. Children who have been sexually abused often struggle with promiscuity as they mature. Being used for sexual gratification teaches children, among other things, that they have no separateness as individuals, destroying the foundation needed to build healthy boundaries. This heinous act creates vulnerable children who grow into vulnerable teenagers and adults.

▶ Those who have been victims of abuse, including rape and incest, often feel like "damaged goods" and often lower their sexual boundaries.

▶ Those who have experienced a premarital pregnancy typically feel a deep sense of shame and often lower their sexual standards. When sexual boundaries have been broken and the heart has been hurt, the Bible is specific about the comfort of the Lord and the emotional healing He offers.

"The LORD is close to the brokenhearted and saves those who are crushed in spirit." (Psalm 34:18)

7 Lack of **Discretion**

Discretion, the ability to make responsible decisions and to distinguish between right and wrong, between wise and unwise, is sorely needed in children and adults alike. A sexual crisis has invaded our culture, and even if we try to avoid it, every one of us is exposed. The nature of all temptation is fundamentally based on a lie—a lie that promises intimacy but produces only a counterfeit. This counterfeit intimacy promotes a worldview that claims our sexual standards are now dispensable.

However, the book of Proverbs says, *"My son, preserve sound judgment and discernment, do not let them out of your sight"* (Proverbs 3:21).

Subtle seduction calls for both discernment to detect and discretion to decide to avoid the sexual "*hooks*" that are most apparent in these three areas:

1. **Sexually-driven advertising** can manipulate our thinking and condition us to accept a lower moral standard.

   "Their idea of pleasure is to carouse in broad daylight. They are ... reveling in their pleasures while they feast with you. With eyes full of adultery, they never stop sinning." (2 Peter 2:13–14)

2. **Television programming** usually has as a standard sexual theme: illicit sexual relationships, extramarital affairs, the false delights of homosexual relationships, and even teenage sexual activity.

   "They have left the straight way and wandered off to follow the way of Balaam son of Beor, who loved the wages of wickedness. ... These men are springs without water and mists driven by a storm. Blackest darkness is reserved for them. For they mouth empty, boastful words and, by appealing to the lustful desires of sinful human nature, they entice people who are just escaping from those who live in error. They promise them freedom, while

they themselves are slaves of depravity—for a man is a slave to whatever has mastered him." (2 Peter 2:15, 17–19)

3. **The Internet** has had a worldwide impact and has quickly become indispensable to education, business, and professions. But just as with all good things, the enemy of our souls is looking for innocent prey to devour. In the privacy of our homes, the Internet offers the most perverted sexual enticements ever known, stimulating the brain as powerfully as cocaine. As the fastest-growing addiction today, pornography takes a terrible toll on our minds and on our marriages.

"Be self-controlled and alert. Your enemy the devil prowls around like a roaring lion looking for someone to devour. Resist him, standing firm in the faith, because you know that your brothers throughout the world are undergoing the same kind of sufferings." (1 Peter 5:8–9)

God intended the sexual relationship for pleasure within the protected confines of marriage. With pleasure as a goal, the number one question asked about sex (outside of marriage) is: "How far is too far?" Or to put it another way, "How close can we get without getting burned?" If the question is: "To what degree can we have any sexual activity outside of marriage?" the Bible's limit is clear: *"Among you there must not be even a hint of sexual immorality"* (Ephesians 5:3).

Fires can burn out gradually or burn out of control. If a sexual fire is smoldering, the natural response is to add more fuel to keep it going. When holding hands or casual kissing no longer arouses the flame of passion, "the law of diminishing returns" kicks in. If passion is the goal, then more intimate sexual activity is needed to reach the same level of pleasure experienced before. This progression is built into us by God and is intended to lead to the culmination of sexual oneness in marriage. Apart from a marriage relationship between a man and a woman, God never ever approves of the culmination of sexual oneness—nor does He condone attempts at sexual arousal. *"It is God's will that you should be sanctified: that you should avoid sexual immorality."* (1 Thessalonians 4:3)

The Progression of Touch[5]

▶ Hugging

▶ Holding hands

▶ Closed-mouth kissing

▶ Open mouth/deep French kissing (Because this simulates the sex act, many conscientious yet-to-be-married couples have declared this off-limits until marriage.)

▶ Bodily kissing

▶ Touching over clothes/bodily caressing/ petting

▶ Touching under clothes/hand to sexual organs

▶ Mutual masturbation/oral sex

▶ Sexual intercourse

"It can't be wrong when it feels so right!" This classic line has been used for years to excuse sexual impurity when passion runs deep. In the progression of touch (from hugging to holding hands to kissing to the ultimate sex act), where do you draw the line? Never underestimate the power of sexual passion! Momentary passion can erode any sound commitment previously made. Even the first steps of physical activity are highly addictive.

Perhaps the best question to ask is: "Which steps can you take and still glorify God?" The best option is to not even start down a progression that could ignite a fire—a fire that cannot be legitimately put out!

> **"Can a man scoop fire into his lap without his clothes being burned?"**
> **(Proverbs 6:27)**

ROOT CAUSE for Not Maintaining Sexual Integrity

We are all created with three inner needs, the need for love, for significance, and for security.[6] When one or more of these needs is not met, we can have a "hole in our heart" that we are trying to fill. That is why so many people find themselves *"looking for love in all the wrong places!"*

WRONG BELIEFS:

▶ Based on **unfulfilled love and security** usually felt by females who think, *Being sexually involved fills my deep need for love and security.*

▶ Based on **unfulfilled significance**, usually felt by males who think, *Being sexually involved gives me a sense of power and control and provides physical release for my sex drive.*

RIGHT BELIEF:

"My deepest needs for love, significance, and security can never be filled through any sexual involvement outside of marriage. I will rely on Jesus to meet my deepest inner needs. He will provide His power so that I can overcome temptation and be a person of sexual integrity."

"His divine power has given us everything we need for life and godliness through our knowledge of him who called us by his own glory and goodness. Through these he has given us his very great and precious promises, so that through them you may participate in the divine nature and escape the corruption in the world caused by evil desires."
(2 Peter 1:3–4)

Sexual intimacy in marriage is a gift from God, but this good gift is often twisted by fallen humanity. In our world, premarital sex, seduction, homosexuality, and extramarital affairs are promoted and sensationalized.

You can find distortions of God's intention for sex everywhere, and sometimes those distortions can be very appealing.

Have you been struggling to defeat a sexual habit or desire but find yourself unable to resist? Integrity begins in your heart. Only through God's power can you live in the purity that He desires for you. Only through His power can you have integrity that lasts.

> "In my integrity you uphold me."
> (Psalm 41:12)

How to Have Integrity That Lasts

If you would like to have sexual integrity in your life, God has a solution for you—a solution that can be spelled out in four points.

#1 God's Purpose for You is *Salvation*.

What was God's motive in sending Christ to earth?

To express His love for you by saving you! The Bible says ...

"God so loved the world that he gave his one and only Son, that whoever believes in him shall not perish but have eternal life. For God did not send his Son into the world to condemn the world, but to save the world through him." (John 3:16–17)

What was Jesus' purpose in coming to earth?

To forgive your sins, empower you to have victory over sin, and enable you to live a fulfilled life! Jesus said ...

"I have come that they may have life, and have it to the full." (John 10:10)

#2 Your Problem is *Sin*.

What exactly is sin?

Sin is living independently of God's standard—knowing what is right, but choosing what is wrong.

The Bible says ...

"Anyone, then, who knows the good he ought to do and doesn't do it, sins." (James 4:17)

What is the major consequence of sin?

Spiritual "death," eternal separation from God. Scripture states ...

"Your iniquities [sins] have separated you from your God." (Isaiah 59:2)

"For the wages of sin is death, but the gift of God is eternal life in Christ Jesus our Lord." (Romans 6:23)

#3 God's Provision for You is the *Savior.*

Can anything remove the penalty for sin?

Yes! Jesus died on the cross to personally pay the penalty for your sins.

"God demonstrates his own love for us in this: While we were still sinners, Christ died for us." (Romans 5:8)

What can keep you from being separated from God?

Belief in (entrusting your life to) Jesus Christ as the only way to God the Father. Jesus says ...

"I am the way and the truth and the life. No one comes to the Father except through me." (John 14:6)

#4 Your Part is *Surrender.*

Give Christ control of your life—entrusting yourself to Him.

"Jesus said to his disciples, 'If anyone would come after me, he must deny himself and take up his cross [die to your own self-rule] and follow me. For whoever wants to save his life will lose it, but whoever loses his life for me will find it. What good will it be for a man if he gains the whole world, yet forfeits his soul?'" (Matthew 16:24–26)

Place your faith in (rely on) Jesus Christ as your personal Lord and Savior and reject your "good works" as a means of earning God's approval.

"It is by grace you have been saved, through faith—and this not from yourselves, it is the gift of God—not by works, so that no one can boast." (Ephesians 2:8–9)

The moment you choose to receive Jesus as your Lord and Savior—entrusting your life to Him—He comes to live inside you. Then He gives you His power to live the fulfilled life God has planned for you.

If you want to be fully forgiven by God and become the person God created you to be, you can tell Him in a simple, heartfelt prayer like this:

PRAYER OF SALVATION

God, I want a real relationship with You.
I admit that many times I've failed
to go Your way and instead
chosen to go my own way.
Please forgive me for my sins.
Jesus, thank You for dying on the cross
to pay the penalty for my sins
and for rising from the dead to
provide new life.
Come into my life to be my Lord
and my Savior.
Place Your hope in my heart and teach
me to put my confidence in You.
Make me the person
You created me to be.
In Your holy name I pray. Amen.

What Can You Expect Now?

If you sincerely prayed this prayer, look what God says about you!

"To all who received him, to those who believed in his name, he gave the right to become children of God—children born not of natural descent, nor of human decision or a husband's will, but born of God." (John 1:12–13)

STEPS TO SOLUTION

If only Samson had steered clear of sexually immoral women! If only he had committed himself to God's principles of sexual purity! Then he would not have been burned—he would have escaped the trap set for him. But he thought his physical strength would protect him. He thought he could "sleep with the enemy" and not be ensnared. If only he had listened to his parents and had not become entangled with an unbeliever!

If only he had selected a woman of spiritual strength! Rather than following in the footsteps of Samson, recognize that your strength comes from yielding your life to the Lord. You can experience extraordinary spiritual strength by fleeing sexual temptation—and maintaining sexual integrity.

> "Flee from all this, and pursue righteousness, godliness, faith, love, endurance and gentleness."
> (1 Timothy 6:11)

Key Passage to Read

1 Thessalonians 4:3–8

"It is God's will that you should be sanctified: that you should avoid sexual immorality that each of you should learn to control his own body in a way that is holy and honorable, not in passionate lust like the heathen, who do not know God; and that in this matter no one should wrong his brother or take advantage of him. The Lord will punish men for all such sins, as we have already told you and warned you. For God did not call us to be impure, but to live a holy life. Therefore, he who rejects this instruction does not reject man but God, who gives you his Holy Spirit."

- ▶ God calls **you** to be holy—literally set apart from the world's thinking. (v. 3)

- ▶ God calls **you** to sexual integrity. (v. 3)

- ▶ God calls **you** to control your sexual desires. (v. 4)

- ▶ God calls **you** to be holy and honorable. (v. 4)

- ▶ God condemns **your** lust. (v. 5)

- ▶ God holds **you** accountable for your treatment of others. (v. 6)

- ▶ God will punish **your** promiscuity. (v. 6)

- ▶ God does not call **you** to be impure. (v. 7)

- ▶ God calls **you** to live a holy life. (v. 7)

- ▶ God sees **your** involvement in sexual sin as rejection of Him. (v. 8)

Right now you can live by faith—or you can live by your feelings. One way leads to spiritual life—the other leads to spiritual death.

Do you have a Delilah in your life—someone who uses your romantic relationship to try to control you? Delilah used a classic line: "If you love me, prove it." Her plea was dripping with sensual passion.

> *"She said to him, 'How can you say, "I love you," when you won't confide in me? This is the third time you have made a fool of me and haven't told me the secret of your great strength.' With such nagging she prodded him day after day until he was tired to death."* (Judges 16:15–16)

Samson fell for Delilah's manipulation and, ultimately, fell out of God's favor. As a result, he lost both his strength and his sight because, actually, all along he had no spiritual insight.

Are you a modern day Samson who doesn't know how to respond to the pressure of sexual temptation? Are you caught in a dilemma of being both drawn to and pressured by someone? If you find yourself lacking sexual integrity, without right responses when the coercion begins, learn what to say when you don't know what to say! The Bible says ...

**"Apply your heart to instruction
and your ears to words of knowledge."
(Proverbs 23:12)**

Top Twenty Enticements

1 **"Everybody's doing it."**

"Then it won't be hard to find someone else to do it."

2 **"It's okay because we really love each other."**

"If we really love each other, we'll do what's best for each other and sex outside marriage isn't best for either of us."

3 **"I promise not to tell anyone if you'll have sex with me."**

"No promise is necessary because there won't be anything to tell. I would regret having sex whether or not anyone else knew."

4 **"Sex is fun—nothing bad will happen."**

"Sex is serious—you can't guarantee what will happen."

5 **"I know what I want."**

"I know what I want too—I want to save myself for the one I'll marry."

6 **"What are you afraid of?"**

"About 25 sexually transmitted diseases (STDs) and the possibility of pregnancy."

7 **"There's nothing wrong with us having sex."**

"If there's nothing wrong, then why do we have to sneak around?"

8 **"If you love me, you'll let me."**

"If you loved me, you wouldn't ask me."

9 **"What's wrong with you?"**

"No, it's what's right for me and for you. It's right for both of us to protect our future."

10 **"Now's the right time to make love."**

"The only right time to make love is when we're both married to the right people."

11 **"Make love to me—I know you want me."**

"Whether I want you or not, I want what God wants more."

12 **"Sex is just a game."**

"If sex is just a game, that means someone loses and I don't want to play."

13 **"After all I've done for you, you owe me sex."**

"I don't owe anyone sex."

14 **"I'll protect you—I'll use a condom."**

"A condom can't protect my conscience, and it won't protect my heart."

15 **"If you don't put out—then get out."**

"Then I'm getting out."

16 **"If you were a real man, you would do it!"**

"If you were a real friend, you wouldn't say that."

17 **"You owe me a reason for saying no."**

"I don't owe you a reason—we both have the right to say no."

18 **"You're a chicken."**

"It takes more strength to abstain than to give in."

19 **"I thought you loved me."**

"I love you so much that I don't want to sin against you or against God."

20 **"No one will ever know."**

"I'll know, you'll know, and most importantly, God will know."

"Nothing in all creation is hidden from God's sight. Everything is uncovered and laid bare before the eyes of him to whom we must give account." (Hebrews 4:13)

Refuse to allow verbal pressure tactics to violate your values. Such a violation will keep you from experiencing God's best for your life. When people appeal to your natural sexual desires, decide not to let your defenses down. Just one unguarded mistake, just one failure to resist an enticement can change your life forever. The Bible says, *"They mouth empty, boastful words and, by appealing to the lustful desires of sinful human nature, they entice people who are just escaping from those who live in error"* (2 Peter 2:18).

WHAT ARE Seven Myths about Sex?

As a rule, people believe what they want to believe, and in no other area could this be truer than with sex. Many people believe they can have indiscriminate sex without any consequences. Or, to put it another way, they "sow their wild oats," and then pray for crop failure![7]

But the Bible says ...

> **"Do not be deceived: God cannot be mocked. A man reaps what he sows."**
> **(Galatians 6:7)**

1. **Myth**: "All is fair in love and war."

   Truth: The basis of love is sacrifice, not fairness.

   "This is how we know what love is: Jesus Christ laid down his life for us. And we ought to lay down our lives for our brothers." (1 John 3:16)

2. **Myth**: "If it feels good, it must be good."

   Truth: Sin can feel good, but that doesn't mean sin is good.

   "He whose walk is blameless is kept safe, but he whose ways are perverse will suddenly fall." (Proverbs 28:18)

3. **Myth**: "I need sex in order to feel good about myself."

   Truth: Real love is not self-seeking.

   "[Love] is not rude, it is not self-seeking." (1 Corinthians 13:5)

4. **Myth**: "A husband prefers his wife to be sexually experienced."

   Truth: Premarital sex can breed jealousy and distrust in a marriage.

   "Jealousy arouses a husband's fury, and he will show no mercy when he takes revenge." (Proverbs 6:34)

5. Myth: "As long as I'm not married, I should be able to have sex with whomever I want."

Truth: The only instance where God blesses two people in a sexual relationship is within a husband and wife marital relationship.

"'For this reason a man will leave his father and mother and be united to his wife, and the two will become one flesh.' So they are no longer two, but one." (Mark 10:7–8)

6. Myth: "Sexual flirtation is harmless."

Truth: Sexual flirtation harms the conscience and leads to sexual arousal and physical involvement.

"Flee the evil desires of youth, and pursue righteousness, faith, love and peace, along with those who call on the Lord out of a pure heart." (2 Timothy 2:22)

7. Myth: "Multiple sex partners give me more experience."

Truth: Multiple experiences breed comparisons and dissatisfaction.

"Do not share in the sins of others. Keep yourself pure." (1 Timothy 5:22)

We all know the sickening feeling of living with a guilty conscience or knowing we have let others down or knowing we have let God down. The problem is that we were not aiming at the right target. Like Samson, we can be solely focused on self-gratification instead of on self-control. When we place ourselves in dependence on God and when our target is right before God, we can have a clear conscience and be a light in the midst of darkness.

"I strive always to keep my conscience clear before God and man." (Acts 24:16)

▶ **I want God's blessing on my life.**

"I urge you, brothers, in view of God's mercy, to offer your bodies as living sacrifices, holy and pleasing to God—this is your spiritual act of worship." (Romans 12:1)

▶ **I don't want to do anything that will hinder my prayer life with God.**

"If I had cherished sin in my heart, the Lord would not have listened." (Psalm 66:18)

▶ **I don't want God's disfavor on the life of either of us.**

"Do you not know that the wicked will not inherit the kingdom of God? Do not be

deceived: Neither the sexually immoral nor idolaters nor adulterers nor male prostitutes nor homosexual offenders nor thieves nor the greedy nor drunkards nor slanderers nor swindlers will inherit the kingdom of God." (1 Corinthians 6:9–10)

▶ **I don't want to take the place of God by trying to meet all the needs of another person.**

"You shall have no other gods before me." (Deuteronomy 5:7)

▶ **I don't want anyone else to take the place of God in my life.**

"Jesus replied: 'Love the Lord your God with all your heart and with all your soul and with all your mind.'" (Matthew 22:37)

▶ **I want to live a life of integrity, being the same in the dark as I am in the light.**

"I know, my God, that you test the heart and are pleased with integrity." (1 Chronicles 29:17)

▶ **I want others to see the power of Christ in me.**

"His divine power has given us everything we need for life and godliness through our knowledge of him who called us by his own glory and goodness." (2 Peter 1:3)

Because *"I can do everything through him [Christ] who gives me strength"* (Philippians 4:13), I am closing the door to all thoughts of sexual involvement as a means of getting my needs met. The Lord will meet all of my needs.

> "My God will meet all your needs
> according to his glorious riches
> in Christ Jesus."
> (Philippians 4:19)

QUESTION: "I'm a teenage girl and have committed my life to the Lord. What can help me resist sexual temptation?"

ANSWER: Carry visual reminders of your highest ideals, values, and commitments. For example, many young people choose to wear a "purity ring" to symbolize their covenant to the Lord—specifically, to abstain from engaging in sexual activity outside the marriage relationship.

These visual reminders will help you to remain steadfast in your belief that ...

> "Godliness has value for all things,
> holding promise for both the present life
> and the life to come."
> (1 Timothy 4:8)

You cannot take back sexually that which has been given any more than you can take back that which has been spoken.

However, that which has been lost—virginity—can be reclaimed. As you have opened your heart to the Lord and as you have begun to desire His best, you can come to know Him as both Redeemer and Restorer. If you are single and not a virgin, God still desires that you live a life of sexual integrity. He can empower you—if you permit Him—to have victory over the past.

God intends your sexuality to be a wonderful present to your marriage partner. From this point on, save yourself for the one God has saved for you.

"Create in me a pure heart, O God, and renew a steadfast spirit within me. ... I will cleanse you from all your impurities. ... I will give you a new heart and put a new spirit in you. ... I will put my Spirit in you and move you to follow my decrees."
(Psalm 51:10; Ezekiel 36:25–27)

Invest in Integrity

The following is an acrostic on INTEGRITY.

Invite others to walk the road of sexual integrity with you.

▶ Allow yourself to be vulnerable with people whom you can trust.

▶ Share your struggle with a wise and understanding friend or mentor.

▶ Go to a spiritual leader or a support group and ask for accountability. Remember ...

"Two are better than one, because they have a good return for their work: If one falls down, his friend can help him up. But pity the man who falls and has no one to help him up!" (Ecclesiastes 4:9–10)

Never put yourself or your loved one in a tempting situation.

▶ Consider bedrooms off-limits.

▶ Don't be in a home alone with each other.

▶ Know your triggers—know what is sexually tempting to you and make a decision to counter those triggers. Remember ...

"Do not offer the parts of your body to sin, as instruments of wickedness, but rather offer yourselves to God, as those who have

been brought from death to life; and offer the parts of your body to him as instruments of righteousness." (Romans 6:13)

Trust God to meet your need for love.

▶ Don't use sexual pleasure to try to meet your needs for love and affirmation—it won't work!

▶ Learn to live dependent on the Lord. Give Him your heart.

▶ Let Him know that you are looking to Him to be your Need-Meeter.

"Let the morning bring me word of your unfailing love, for I have put my trust in you. Show me the way I should go, for to you I lift up my soul." (Psalm 143:8)

Enjoy others instead of using others.

▶ Don't try to fill up your "love bucket" with sex—there will be holes in that bucket!

▶ Learn to be friends with each other—to enjoy doing many activities with each other.

▶ Realize that a real friend will never use you sexually. Remember ...

"Love must be sincere. Hate what is evil; cling to what is good. Be devoted to one another in brotherly love. Honor one another above yourselves." (Romans 12:9–10)

Give yourself only to sexually pure relationships.

▶ Guard the gift of sexual intimacy until the time you are married.

▶ Keep the gift of sexual intimacy exclusively for your marriage partner.

▶ Realize that you can have an "intimate relationship" that is not a sexual relationship.

"Now that you have purified yourselves by obeying the truth so that you have sincere love for your brothers, love one another deeply, from the heart." (1 Peter 1:22)

Refuse to justify any sexual impurity.

▶ Honestly face the sexual sin in your life.

▶ Pray for God to convict you of any sin.

▶ Commit yourself to being a person of purity. Remember …

"Watch and pray so that you will not fall into temptation. The spirit is willing, but the body is weak." (Matthew 26:41)

Isolate yourself from people who tempt you.

▶ Leave any relationship that does not honor God.

▶ Refuse to be with someone who dabbles in drugs or tries to use alcohol to weaken your will.

▶ State your commitment: "I will not allow myself to be alone with individuals who tempt me sexually." Remember ...

"Do not be misled: 'Bad company corrupts good character.'" (1 Corinthians 15:33)

Transform your mind through the written Word of God.

▶ Find Scripture that is focused on your area of struggle.

▶ Ask God to reprogram your mind as you follow a discipline to read and memorize Scripture.

▶ Read one chapter of Proverbs daily.

"I have hidden your word in my heart that I might not sin against you." (Psalm 119:11)

Yield to Christ, who lives in you, trusting Him to produce in you a life of purity.

▶ Consciously submit your will to the will of Christ when you are tempted—do it *before* you are tempted.

▶ Don't lie to yourself—refuse to be lulled into false confidence in your own ability to withstand temptation.

▶ Live your life dependent on Christ, who lives in you. The Bible says ...

"I have been crucified with Christ and I no longer live, but Christ lives in me. The life I live in the body, I live by faith in the Son of God, who loved me and gave himself for me." (Galatians 2:20)

You can't be fulfilled in the way that God intended unless you are connected to Him, living dependently on Him. If you allow Christ—living in you—to find expression through you, He will empower you to have sexual purity.

How many times have you found yourself in a situation where you should have determined ahead of time how you would respond? Yet in the heat of the moment, you acted and later realized with regret that you had made the wrong decision?

Many decisions need to be made prior to when they are needed. This involves knowing the end result you desire and then, ahead of time, committing yourself to a plan to achieve that desire. In the Bible, Job had such a plan in order to maintain his purity. He made a commitment—a covenant vow before God:

> "I made a covenant with my eyes not to look lustfully at a girl."
> (Job 31:1)

▶ **Write** out your vow to be sexually pure from this day forward.

- Share your pledge with your parents, a special friend, or someone else you trust who knows the Lord.

- Consider matting and framing your commitment.

"When you make a vow to God, do not delay in fulfilling it. He has no pleasure in fools; fulfill your vow." (Ecclesiastes 5:4)

▶ **Find** friends who hold the same commitment.

- Abstaining from sex is easier alongside close friends who honor the same vow.

- Practice the joy of talking to Jesus as a friend.

"I appeal to you ... that you may be perfectly united in mind and thought." (1 Corinthians 1:10)

▶ **Pray** for the right accountability partner.

- Ask someone who cares about you and someone you deeply respect to hold you accountable sexually. Ideally, this person should be several years older, one who will ask candid questions and one who will "speak the truth in love."

- Commit to meeting with this person on a regular basis.

"Wounds from a friend can be trusted, but an enemy multiplies kisses." (Proverbs 27:6)

▶ **Develop** a proactive strategy for countering sexual triggers.

- Don't be alone in your date's home. Don't go into your date's bedroom.

- If your sexual challenge is the Internet, use an Internet filter; if your challenge is sex on TV, use a blocking service.

"Do not set foot on the path of the wicked or walk in the way of evil men." (Proverbs 4:14)

▶ **Make** a list of goals you have for life.

- Develop short-term goals (six months to two years) and long-term goals (two to ten years).

- Tell your family and friends about your goals so that everyone can encourage you in the same direction. Pray for God to put into your heart the work He has planned for you to do.

"We are God's workmanship, created in Christ Jesus to do good works, which God prepared in advance for us to do." (Ephesians 2:10)

▶ **Wear** a purity ring, bracelet, or necklace.

- A physical item can be a spiritual reminder of your commitment to sexual purity. During your wedding ceremony, you can replace your commitment rings with your wedding rings.

- Each of you can give your commitment rings to your parents, expressing appreciation for their encouragement, or the rings can be passed down to your own children as a reminder to them to stay pure.

"Then will I ever sing praise to your name and fulfill my vows day after day." (Psalm 61:8)

▶ **Write** a love letter to your future mate.

- Tell your future marriage partner why you chose to save yourself for him (or her), and share what purity means to you.

- Sign your letter, date it, and then read it once a month.

"Marriage should be honored by all, and the marriage bed kept pure, for God will judge the adulterer and all the sexually immoral." (Hebrews 13:4)

▶ **Lend** a hand in helping others.

- If you are busy, you are less likely to be preoccupied with sex.

- Help an elderly person on a regular basis. Volunteer your time in service to others, possibly at a nursing home, hospital, or shelter for battered women and children.

"Let your light shine before men, that they may see your good deeds and praise your Father in heaven." (Matthew 5:16)

▶ **Rely** on the spiritual beliefs or teachings of your church.

- Almost all churches—and even most world religions—teach the value of maintaining sexual purity.

- Spiritual faith is a strong motivation to do what is right.

"Be on your guard; stand firm in the faith; be men of courage; be strong." (1 Corinthians 16:13)

▶ **Make** a Promise List.

- "I promise I will practice sexual abstinence."

- "I promise I will date only those who are committed to sexual integrity."

- "I promise I will set sexual boundaries and stay within those boundaries."

- "I promise I will not be alone with a date in a bedroom, a parked car, or any other compromising place."

- "I promise I will guard my eyes, my mind, and my heart against sexual impurity."

- "I promise I will not take any drink or drug that would weaken my defenses."

- "I promise I will not look at pornography."

- "I promise I will not visit Internet sex chat rooms."

Personalize this list and read it at least once a week, renewing your vows to the Lord.

"Since we have these promises, dear friends, let us purify ourselves from everything that contaminates body and spirit, perfecting holiness out of reverence for God."
(2 Corinthians 7:1)

Do you want to have the most satisfying sex life possible? Even though you may know that God will not bless a sexual relationship outside of marriage, you may think it doesn't matter. You may believe that God doesn't really care about you, but God cares deeply about you and He cares about what you do. He wants you to be fulfilled in your life. He knows that couples who enter marriage with sexual baggage from the past can have great difficulty coming together with the same trust and respect as can those who have maintained sexual integrity. By saving yourself sexually, you give a priceless wedding gift to your covenant partner—you give your mate the gift of purity.

The Bible says ...

> "[There is] a time to embrace
> and a time to refrain."
> (Ecclesiastes 3:5)

When You Choose to Wait

▶ **Emotionally**—You have ...

- Freedom from guilt

- Freedom from anxiety

- Freedom from grief

- Freedom from emotional scars

"Do not be anxious about anything, but in everything, by prayer and petition, with thanksgiving, present your requests to God. And the peace of God, which transcends all understanding, will guard your hearts and your minds in Christ Jesus." (Philippians 4:6–7)

▶ **Physically**—You have ...

- No premarital pregnancy

- No sexually transmitted disease

- No abortion consequences

"Flee from sexual immorality. All other sins a man commits are outside his body, but he who sins sexually sins against his own body." (1 Corinthians 6:18)

▶ **Socially**—You have ...

- Positive relationships

- Positive self-image

- Positive values

- Positive reputation

"Commit your way to the LORD; trust in him and he will do this: He will make your righteousness shine like the dawn, the justice of your cause like the noonday sun." (Psalm 37:5–6)

▶ **Spiritually**—You have ...

- A pure conscience before God

- A pure vision for God's will

- A pure motive initiated by God

- A pure relationship with God

"Blessed are the pure in heart, for they will see God." (Matthew 5:8)

A sexually transmitted disease (STD) is an infection that is transmitted through sexual activity, whether vaginal, anal, or oral sex or intimate skin-to-skin contact, from one person who is infected to another person.

▶ *Bacterial STDs* can be cured with antibiotics.

▶ *Viral STDs* can never be cured. Symptoms, such as sores or warts, can be treated, but the virus remains in the body, causing the symptoms to flare up again and again.

In the 16th century, syphilis was the only identified venereal disease. Then, in the 19th century, gonorrhea joined syphilis as a cause of infertility. Both were classified as incurable until the discovery of penicillin in 1943, which eradicated venereal diseases (VDs) as a major public health issue. However, the wild, sexual revolution of the 1960s became a breeding ground for a myriad of STDs (the new label), including chlamydia and HPV in 1976 and HIV/AIDS in the early 1980s. Today there are more than 25 STDs.

Do Condoms provide "Safe Sex"?

Would you use a parachute that you know will fail 2 out of every 100 times? The myth of "safe" sex is not only dangerous, but also life-threatening. To think that condoms can guarantee safe sex is woefully misleading. Every 2 to 4 condoms out of 100 slip down, slip off, leak, or break. Sex can be considered "safe" only when practiced within the guidelines established by God. Sex joins two people in a unified relationship, forming a unique bond where two truly *become one flesh* (Genesis 2:24). A condom does not prevent that bonding, which is anything but "casual."

Additionally, condoms provide only limited protection against sexually transmitted diseases and must be used both correctly and consistently to be an effective form of protection from pregnancy. However, studies show that condoms are properly used only 50% of the time.[9]

Unlike condoms, which reduce only a small percentage of the risks, abstinence is the only true "safe" method—eliminating 100% of the risks!

True love protects 100% of the time. Ultimately, abstinence is an act of true love that protects every part of a person—body, soul, and spirit.

The Bible says ...

> "Discretion will protect you, and
> understanding will guard you."
> (Proverbs 2:11)

The Myth of Safe Sex with Condoms[10]

▶ **Pregnancy**

Condoms reduce the risk of pregnancy by only 86% during the first year of use.

▶ **HPV** (Human Papilloma Virus)

Condoms reduce the risk of contracting HPV by around 50%.

▶ **Syphilis**

Condoms reduce the risk of syphilis by more than 50% if used 100% of the time.

▶ **Chlamydia and Gonorrhea**

Condoms reduce the risk of these two sexually transmitted diseases (STDs) by less than 50% if used 100% of the time.

▶ **Genital herpes** (HSV-2)

Condoms reduce the risk of herpes by less than 50%.

▶**HIV/AIDS** (Human immunodeficiency virus [HIV] is what causes acquired immunodeficiency syndrome [AIDS])

Condoms reduce the risk of HIV by only 85% if used 100% of the time.

When people are seduced by the myth of safe sex, they are more likely to engage in dangerous behavior and in heterosexual and homosexual experimentation.

Don't be lulled by the lie of "complete condom protection." The only safe sex is a committed sexual relationship with a lifelong marriage partner. Physical purity is necessary for spiritual purity.

"Have nothing to do with godless myths ... rather, train yourself to be godly."
(1 Timothy 4:7)

When you have sexual integrity
—no matter what others do or don't
do, no matter the pressure or pull—
you will do what is right in God's sight,
you will stay sexually pure.

—June Hunt

SCRIPTURES TO MEMORIZE

Why do I need to **learn to control** my sexual urges?

*"It is God's will that you should be sanctified: that you should avoid sexual immorality; that each of you should **learn to control** his own body in a way that is holy and honorable, not in passionate lust like the heathen, who do not know God."*
(1 Thessalonians 4:3–5)

Is there any difference between **sexual sins** and **other sins**?

*"Flee from sexual immorality. All **other sins** a man commits are outside his body, but he who sins **sexually sins** against his own body."* (1 Corinthians 6:18)

Although the Bible says, *"You are not your own,"* isn't what you do with **your body** your own business?

*"Do you not know that your body is a temple of the Holy Spirit, who is in you, whom you have received from God? You are not your own; you were bought at a price. Therefore honor God with **your body**."*
(1 Corinthians 6:19–20)

Sexually, what does **God call us** to do?

*"**God** did not **call us** to be impure, but to live a holy life."* (1 Thessalonians 4:7)

What difference does it make if I have sex outside of marriage—I'm not afraid of **being burned**!

*"Can a man scoop fire into his lap without his clothes **being burned?**"* (Proverbs 6:27)

Why should the **marriage bed** be **kept pure**?

*"Marriage should be honored by all, and the **marriage bed kept pure**, for God will judge the adulterer and all the sexually immoral."* (Hebrews 13:4)

What does the Bible say about a person **who commits adultery**?

*"A man **who commits adultery** lacks judgment; whoever does so destroys himself."* (Proverbs 6:32)

Why must **there not be even a hint of sexual immorality**?

*"Among you **there must not be even a hint of sexual immorality**, or of any kind of impurity, or of greed, because these are improper for God's holy people."* (Ephesians 5:3)

Though I've been called "*sexually immoral*," what difference does that make? I'll still **inherit the kingdom of God**.

> "*Do you not know that the wicked will not inherit the kingdom of God? Do not be deceived: Neither the **sexually immoral** nor idolaters nor adulterers nor male prostitutes nor homosexual offenders ... will **inherit the kingdom of God**.*" (1 Corinthians 6:9–10)

What does it mean: *A man reaps what he sows*?

> "*Do not be deceived: God cannot be mocked. **A man reaps what he sows**. The one who sows to please his sinful nature, from that nature will reap destruction; the one who sows to please the Spirit, from the Spirit will reap eternal life.*" (Galatians 6:7–8)

NOTES

1. W. E. Vine, Merrill F. Unger, and William White, *Vine's Complete Expository Dictionary of Biblical Words*, electronic ed. (Nashville: Thomas Nelson, 1996).

2. Vine, Unger, and White, *Vine's Complete Expository Dictionary of Biblical Words*.

3. Richard Whitaker, *Whitaker's Revised BDB Hebrew-English Lexicon*, BibleWorks 6.0 (2003), electronic edition (Norfolk, VA: BibleWorks, 1995).

4. Vine, Unger, and White, *Vine's Complete Expository Dictionary of Biblical Words*.

5. Nancy Van Pelt, "Straight Talk About Sexual Purity," (n.p.: Hope for the Family), http://www.lovetakestime.com/art-straighttalk.html.

6. Lawrence J. Crabb, Jr., *Understanding People: Deep Longings for Relationship*, Ministry Resources Library (Grand Rapids: Zondervan, 1987), 15–16; Robert S. McGee, *The Search for Significance*, 2nd ed. (Houston, TX: Rapha, 1990), 27–30.

7. Fred Allen, "Fred Allen Quotes," http://fredallen.org/fred-allen-quotes.html.

8. Marilyn Morris, *ABC's of the Birds and Bees for Parents of Toddlers to Teens*, 2nd ed. (Dallas: Charles River, 2000), 297–300. Used by permission.

9. The Medical Institute, "What is Meant by Consistent Condom Use?" edited by Jennifer Shuford, 2008, http://www.medinstitute.org/public/123.cfm.

10. Morris, *Teens, Sex and Choices*, 141–143. Used by permission; The Medical Institute for Sexual Health, "Condoms and STDs," 2003, The Medical Institute, http://www.medinstitute.org/medical/STD%20overview/Condoms&STDs.htm and National Institute of Allergy and Infectious Diseases, National Institute of Health, *Workshop Summary: Scientific Evidence on Condom Effectiveness or Sexually Transmitted Disease (STD) Prevention* (Washington, D.C.: Department of Health and Human Services), presented in Herndon, Virginia, July 2000.

SELECTED BIBLIOGRAPHY

Aim for Success. *Staff Development and Community Leadership Manual*. Dallas: Aim for Success, 2004.

Anderson, Neil T., and Dave Park. *Purity Under Pressure*. Eugene, OR: Harvest House, 1995.

Crabb, Lawrence J., Jr. *Understanding People: Deep Longings for Relationship*. Ministry Resources Library. Grand Rapids: Zondervan, 1987.

Hunt, June. *Bonding with Your Teen through Boundaries*. Nashville, TN: Broadman & Holman Publishers, 2001.

Hunt, June. *Counseling Through Your Bible Handbook*. Eugene, Oregon: Harvest House Publishers, 2008.

Hunt, June. *How to Forgive ... When You Don't Feel Like It*. Eugene, Oregon: Harvest House Publishers, 2007.

Hunt, June. *How to Handle Your Emotions*. Eugene, Oregon: Harvest House Publishers, 2008.

Hunt, June. *Seeing Yourself Through God's Eyes*. Eugene, Oregon: Harvest House Publishers, 2008.

Is Sex Safe? A Look at: Sexually Transmitted Diseases (STDs). Boise, ID: Grapevine, 1997.

McGee, Robert S. *The Search for Significance*. 2nd ed. Houston, TX: Rapha, 1990.

Morris, Marilyn. *ABC's of the Birds and Bees for Parents of Toddlers to Teens*. 2nd ed. Dallas: Charles River, 2000.

Morris, Marilyn. *Choices that Lead to Lifelong Success*. Dallas: Charles River, 1998.

Morris, Marilyn. *Teens, Sex and Choices*. 3rd ed. Dallas: Charles River, 2004.

Van Pelt, Nancy. "Straight Talk About Sexual Purity." Hope for the Family. http://www.lovetakestime.com/art-straighttalk.html.

White, John. *Eros Redeemed: Breaking the Stranglehold of Sexual Sin*. Downers Grove, IL: InterVarsity, 1993.

June Hunt's HOPE FOR THE HEART minibooks are biblically-based, and full of practical advice that is relevant, spiritually-fulfilling and wholesome.

HOPE FOR THE HEART TITLES

www.aspirepress.com

The HOPE FOR THE HEART Biblical Counseling Library is Your Solution!

- Easy-to-read, perfect for anyone.
- Short. Only 96 pages. Good for the busy person.
- Christ-centered biblical advice and practical help
- Tested and proven over 20 years of June Hunt's radio ministry
- 30 titles in the series – each tackling a key issue people face today.
- Affordable. You or your church can give away, lend, or sell them.

Display available for churches and ministries.

www.aspirepress.com